LOTUS ELAN

LOTUS ELAN

Duncan Wherrett

First published in Great Britain in 1993
by Osprey, an imprint of Reed Consumer
Books Limited, Michelin House, 81 Fulham
Road London SW3 6RB and Auckland,
Melbourne, Singapore and Toronto

ISBN 1 85532 377 X

Editor Shaun Barrington
Page design by Paul Kime/Ward Peacock
Partnership
Printed in Hong Kong

Front cover
*1970 Sprint, with the big-valve engine:
basically, an uprated S4 introduced to
extend the production life of the Elan.
The increase in power required other
modifications. The differential and drive
shafts were strengthened, and a
reinforcing bracket was added to the
upper final drive mountings to cope with
the extra torque. The Rotoflex doughnut
joints were also stiffened, which reduced
some of the surge motion caused by
rapid acceleration*

Back cover
*Cornering with élan: normal racing
modifications such as wider tyres, anti-
roll bars front and rear, and adjustable
suspension improve the already fine
handling and stability of the Elan.*

Half-title page
*After being discarded for a period in the
mid 1980s, this traditional bonnet
badge was back on the new Elan and
appears on all current Lotus models*

Title page
*Longer and wider to accommodate 2+2
seating, the Plus 2 was the family man's
Elan. The Plus 2 appeared in 1967 and
was the last Lotus model to be available
in component form. Launched in 1972,
the ultimate Elan was the Plus 2S 130/5
(a regency red example is pictured
here), which combined a five-speed
gearbox with the 126 bhp big-valve
engine*

Right
*A mixed bag of Elans, new and old. The
new Elan did not disappoint its
customers: build quality was excellent (a
welcome change from the original
models), and the car's brilliant handling
had to experienced to be believed.
Although the car did not have the
rugged fun of the old Elan, its quietness
and refinement minimised driver fatigue
on long journeys*

Acknowledgements

I should like to thank the following individuals and companies for their tremendous help and co-operation in making their cars and facilities available for photography during the preparation of this book: John Beaumont; Paul Beedham; Simon Bloomfield; Steven Case; Evets Classic Cars, Derby; Derek Harrison; Max Harvey; Barrie Lansdale; Gary Marshall; Paul Matty Sports Cars, Bromsgrove, Worcester; Mick Miller, Saxmundham, Suffolk; Roy Palmer; Quorn Engine Developments, Quorn, Leicester; Malcolm Ricketts; Michael Rouse; Nick Rouse; SMS, Holbeach, Lincoln; Pat Thomas; Tony Thompson Racing, Melton Mowbray, Leicester; Paula Thorpe; Robert Tracey; Neil Widdowson. Thanks in particular to Richard Wilson for repeated opportunities to photograph his Sprint during its restoration and for checking the text. Finally, Mark Hughes' exellent account of the design development and production of the new Elan (Lotus Elan, ISBN 185532 194 7, published by Osprey at £25 in 1992), was an invaluable source of information.

Contents

Left
In October 1970, what was to be the top of the range Elan appeared – the Sprint. Dreaming up the Sprint proved to be an effective idea in boosting the flagging sales of the S4

The first Elans

The background of Lotus cars has always been very much in racing and the development of sophisticated sports and racing cars. Launched in 1957, the Elite was designed for racing and ordinary motoring and became the first practical road car produced by the Lotus company. It owed much to the knowledge that Lotus' chief Colin Chapman and his colleagues had accumulated during track experience. The styling of the Elite was quite distinctive and made a tremendous impression on the motoring public. The suspension was similar to that developed for the race track and helped give the car extremely good road holding. Powered by a lightweight aluminium 1216 cc Coventry Climax engine giving up to 95 bhp, performance was impressive. The body/chassis unit was of glassfibre monocoque construction and weighed a mere 10½ cwt. The car had a fine racing record, including six consecutive class wins at Le Mans. But although it gave the company a higher public profile, as a design the Elite possessed some inherent shortcomings. The body was made from six mouldings and proved complicated and expensive to manufacture. As a result, Elites were continually produced at a loss.

It was to overcome some of these problems that the Elan was developed. Originally, plans were made for a 2+2 model with a glassfibre monocoque formed in a single mould. In the end, the body was made in two sections, the top part of the body and the floor being bonded together in the curing process. Metal strengthening and over 100 metal fixtures were bonded into the glassfibre during production. The resulting body shell was both light and strong. In typically innovative fashion, Lotus decided to abandon the normal concept of a chassis in favour of their own central 'backbone' version. Initially conceived as a test bed for engines, suspension systems and brakes, the new design proved to be some six times stronger than a conventional chassis, as well as being

Right

The Elite was Lotus's first venture in the open market. It had eye-catching looks and performance to match. The smooth aerodynamic lines of the Elite gave it an exceptional drag co-efficient of 0.29, and its appearance was attractive and quite unique. Although not in wide circulation, the Elite had some enthusiastic support both on and off the track. Due to its double-skinned body with six mouldings, the Elite was time consuming and expensive to manufacture. Some 1030 Elites are thought to have been made; production quality varied and it was never a profitable car. This model is in BMC ivory – the silver roof denotes Special Equipment specification

Above

The Elan was an instant hit with the public when it was launched at the Earls Court Motor Show in October 1962. Remarkably neat in appearance and exhilarating to drive, it was also considerably more practical than many of its contemporaries. Proud owner Derek Harrison bought his carnival red Series 1 as a kit in 1963; he obviously made a pretty good job of assembling the car because it is still in regular use today

Right

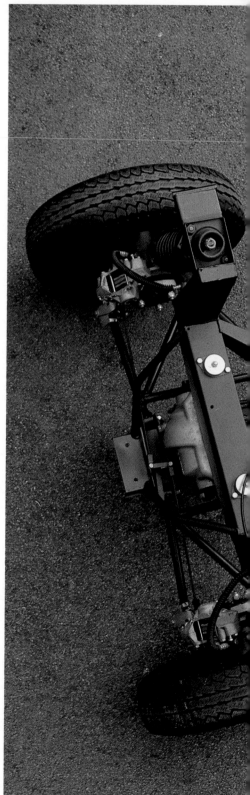

The unique backbone chassis was originally created to test the Elan's suspension and drive train, as the project was being seriously delayed by problems in finalising the design of the all-plastic monocoque. Complete production tooling was needed to produce the necessary moulding, but Lotus was getting nowhere fast. The 'stop-gap' backbone chassis proved to be easy to make and its strength, rigidity and handling qualities surprised even the designers. After Chapman was informed that the backbone chassis could be built for as little as £10 a copy, plans to switch to the still non-existent glassfibre monocoque at a later date were dropped, allowing testing of the Elan prototype to begin in earnest. The backbone chassis was pressed out of 18g sheet steel, reinforced in central areas and drilled for lightness; it weighed a mere 75 lb. (Interestingly, the chassis designer of the 1980's Elan, Jerry Booen, decided to use a refined version of the backbone chassis for the car after experiments with all-composite structures revealed inadequate torsional stiffness.) The final drive and differential housing were rubber mounted. Unfortunately, any oil leaks would perish the lower rubber mounting, putting extra strain on the upper mounting – one of the S1's niggling design faults

light and cheap to make. The success of the backbone chassis ensured its place on all future Lotus models.

The Elan was launched in October 1962, either as a complete car or in kit form, with a free factory check. In component form, the Elan was not subject to purchase tax and could be bought for £1095 – a price which also reflected the lack of assembly costs at the factory. Customers who preferred to buy a complete car could drive one away from the showroom for £1499.

Designed as a thoroughly practical car, the Elan was praised for its smooth-running, yet it lacked the grace and style of the earlier Elite. But its combination of pure chic and high performance caught the mood of the 'swinging sixties' and the imagination of the motoring world. Tremendous fun to drive, the Elan was undoubtedly one of the safest handling of all sports cars.

Production of the S1 and S2 Elan totalled about 900 and 1250 respectively.

Right
The principal designer of the Elan was Ron Hickman, who joined Lotus full-time in 1958 after working for the Ford Motor Co as a styling modeller and development engineer. While still at Ford, Hickman had helped to style the Elite and his rapport with the inspirational Colin Chapman was destined to produce Lotus's most successful car – the Elan. Hickman made his fortune by inventing the 'Workmate' workbench, which Black & Decker subsequently marketed worldwide

Above

The floor and wheel arches were one moulding and the upper section was another – the two being bonded together during production. The body had to be strong enough to take the weight of two people and luggage. Metal inserts were bonded in the glassfibre in order to attach such items as the doors, battery and seats. Steel wire reinforcing frames were bonded in the sill area to give added strength. In addition, 16 bobbins were moulded in to fix the body to the chassis. Although the seats had a fixed back angle, they offered considerable forward and back adjustment and gave good lateral support. The seats were designed to rise as they moved forward to give shorter drivers a better view through the windscreen

Right

The power unit was based on the four-cylinder 116E engine of the Ford Cortina Classic; it had five main bearings and was originally of 1498 cc. Chapman wanted the engine to have twin overhead camshafts. An aluminium alloy head was designed by Richard Ansdale and Harry Mundy, then technical editor of Autocar, who had earlier been responsible for the Coventry Climax engine installed in the Elite. The resulting engine had a compression ratio of 9.5:1 giving 100 bhp at 5700 rpm and 102 lb/ft torque at 4500 rpm. Fitted with two twin-choke Weber 40 DCOE carburettors and a full-synchromesh gearbox, the engine was smooth in operation with a good power curve throughout. The carburettors were rubber mounted to stop the fuel from frothing and weakening the mixture. The original Ford camshaft gear was retained to drive the distributor, fuel and oil pumps. The early die-cast heads were machined by J A Prestwick (JAP). In due course, the jigs and tools were moved to the Lotus plant at Hethel in Norfolk, and the later heads were sand cast. The gearbox came from Ford with Lotus semi-close ratios; the differential was mounted on the chassis

Above

The Elan was the first Lotus sports car to be put into volume production and soon impressed people with its fine handling and high fun factor. The tan seats, as seen here, are extremely rare. As part of Lotus's policy of continually improvement, the engine capacity was increased to 1558 cc in May 1963, to put it within the 1600 cc capacity for racing. All previous 22 Elans with the smaller unit were recalled to have the larger engine retrofitted. Power was boosted to 105 bhp and torque increased to 108 lb/ft; 0-60 now took just 8 seconds and the standing quarter mile 16 seconds. The final drive ratio was 3.9:1, which gave good acceleration, although a 3.55:1 ratio was always an option. The great appeal of driving the Elan on the open road was the sensation of speed and the sheer excitement it engendered. Maximum speed was more than 110 mph; with a little restraint, fuel consumption was a respectable 26 mpg. As a precaution against over-enthusiastic drivers, a rev-limiter was fitted to the distributor rotor arm to cut the ignition at 6500 rpm

Right

The initials of Anthony Colin Bruce Chapman are incorporated in the bonnet badge. The early badges had thinner lettering than the later examples. Born on 19 May 1928, Colin Chapman built the Mk I Lotus from a 1930 Austin Seven in about 1947. Team Lotus entered its first grand prix at Monaco in May 1958, while Group Lotus made its name with the minimalist (in everything except performance) Lotus Seven kit car and went on to produce the Elite, Elan, Europa (or Type 47), new Elite, Esprit, Eclat and Excel sports cars. Regarded by many of his contemporaries as a design genius, Chapman was also a charismatic individual who seemed to live life to the full. Sadly, the colossal pressures involved in saving the recession-hit Group Lotus, and the emerging scandal of his deals with John de Lorean, and the alleged (but unproven) supply of hi-tech information to Eastern Europe, almost certainly contributed to his fatal heart attack on 16 December 1982

Above

From the start, a large number of components were used from other cars. Being a low volume manufacturer, it would have been imprudent for Lotus to produce everything themselves. In Mark Hughes' book on the new Elan (published by Osprey in 1992), designer Ron Hickman recalled: 'The first design for what evolved into the Elan used Sprite body parts, like the windscreen and bumpers, for economy. Even in those days, the tooling cost for a pair of bumpers was, I believe, £30,000. To put that into perspective, the whole Elan project was designed, developed and tooled up, engine included, for £27,000. It was vital for us to beg, steal and borrow parts from any possible source. Bumpers, because they are such heavy metal to shape, require particularly expensive tooling'. Today, it is not clear from which car the boot hinges and door handles came on the S1. In fact, it has become impossible to say what is a definitive standard item, because Lotus would temporarily change an item depending on what was available

Right

The rear lights featured twin reflectors, although early American models had three. The flat boot lid tended to leak water into the boot. However, if the owner kept the drain holes clear and fitted good seals, the boot would stay dry

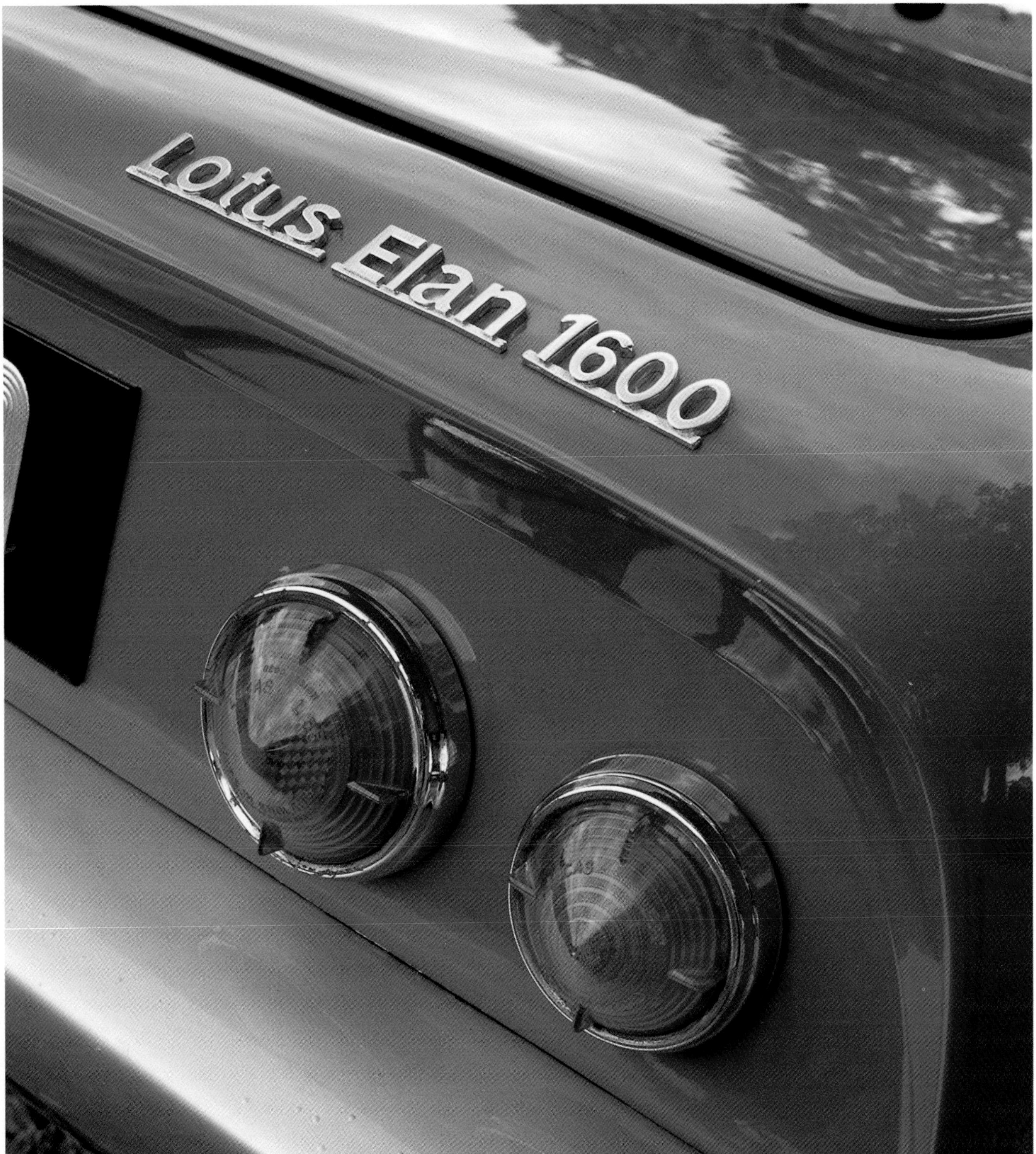
Lotus Elan 1600

Above

Simple and clear, the dashboard was made of oiled teak plywood. With features like a rev-counter, cigarette lighter and independent panel light, the car's interior impressed potential customers. The glove box was open, and had the habit of tipping out its contents, particularly when the car was accelerating hard or cornering at speed. The rack and pinion steering came from the Triumph Vitesse, with modifications, while the telescopic column came from the Herald. The handbrake was under the dash and rather difficult to use, especially if the driver was wearing the static seat belt provided. The handbrake also required regular adjustment and maintenance

Above

On early Elans, the doors were opened with a simple cord pull, which was quickly changed to a handle. This example has its original vinyl trim from 1963. The wide doors made access relatively easy although inadequate seals caused leaks when driving in the rain. Vinyl seats and carpet, including the luggage section behind the seats, completed the interior. The sliding windows had spring counterbalance weights inside

Above

The hood was PVC fabric and took some minutes to assemble. Two large side frames were installed first, followed by two joining supports. The hood was then stretched over the top. When erected, it made travelling at speed a noisy business and was not particularly watertight. Most owners preferred to keep the roof stored away in the boot

Above left

The fully independent suspension system was a significant factor in the handling qualities of the Elan. Developed from racing experience, it was similar to the Elite's, although the parts were not interchangeable. The front suspension had double pressed steel wishbones, a co-axial coil spring/damper and an anti-roll bar

Above right

The rear suspension featured a long telescopic shock absorber inside coil springs. The shock absorbers and springs were flexibly mounted in rubber 'Lotocones' at the top end. A single wide-angled lower wishbone was attached to the base of the hub

carrier and fixed to the chassis with metal and rubber bushes. In order to fully exploit the Elan's handling potential, these rubber bushes had to be kept in good order. With hard driving and kerb hitting, bent wishbones were not uncommon. Consequently, the suspension really needed to be overhauled after about 20,000 miles. Drain holes were put in the chassis and any blockage of these would lead to corrosion. The Elan's braking system was absolutely first class – 9½ inch Girling discs were fitted on the front with 10 inch on the rear, balanced 51 and 49 per cent respectively. As the Elan weighed only 13¼ cwt, racing drivers had little difficulty in out-braking competitors on the track. The final drive is not fitted in this photograph

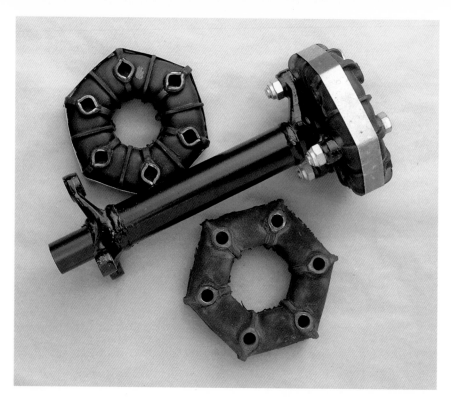

Above

The famous and infamous Rotoflex rubber couplings. In an arrangement originally
designed by Chapman for the Lotus 21 Formula One car of 1961, the articulated half-
shafts had rubber universal joints, or 'doughnuts', at each end, making four in all.
These rubber couplings were favoured over metal splines in the drive shafts because
they absorbed stress and lateral movement more successfully, cushioning the
transmission in general and making the differential less susceptible to road shocks.
The doughnuts did, however, cause a certain amount of extra surging motion under
hard acceleration that took a little getting used to. The picture shows a later drive
shaft with an extension piece. Should the doughnut fail, this prevented the shaft from
flailing about. Both the early and later doughnuts are shown here – the later version
having extra metal inserts for greater stability. Derived from Hillman Imp units, these
rubber couplings have been much maligned, but with proper, smooth driving and
regular inspections they were quite capable of giving many thousands of miles of good
service

Right

Another popular colour was Lotus yellow. Simon Bloomfield uses his S1 as much on
the track as off it. Although standard practice would be for the lower part of the sill to
be black and the wheels silver, Simon prefers this colour scheme. The early wheels
were steel and attached with four bolts under the hub caps. Radials soon replaced the
early cross-ply tyres

Above

November 1964 saw the introduction of the S2. The basic car hardly changed throughout the range, but there were a number of changes in detail, such as different door handles, smaller pedals and a quick release fuel cap. Knock-on centre-lock wheels were an optional extra. With larger front caliper pistons and an improved master cylinder, the brakes were even more effective on the S2

Right

A rear light cluster rather than the individual lights was now fitted. The bases for the lights were made of chromed zinc die castings; if they become pitted, it is not possible to have them rechromed successfully. Many owners prefer to keep the original items, even if they are not perfect, rather than use a new component

Above

The bumpers were made of glassfibre and filled with polyurethane foam. This made them very resilient to small impacts and easy to repair. The standard colour for the bumpers was silver, known as silver fox, although a few demonstration cars were finished with chrome bumpers. The pods for the retractable or 'pop-up' headlights were vacuum operated; Californian road safety laws demanded that the centre of the headlights had to be two feet from the ground when raised

Right

The dashboard layout changed little in the S2. The glove compartment was now lockable and the wood varnished rather than oiled – a touch of class

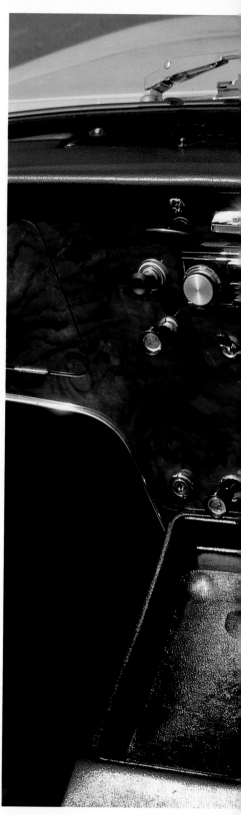

Series 3 and Series 4

As with any manufacturer, for a model to remain viable it is necessary for constant improvements to be made. Even though they were popular and successful, the early Elans were very basic cars in terms of equipment and trim. To build on the Elan's past sales success and broaden its popularity, Lotus introduced the improved Series 3 in late 1965. Previously, the Elan had only been available in drophead form. A separate hard top could be purchased from the factory to give a warmer, drier ride but this was neither easy nor quick to fit. The new fixed head coupe overcame these shortcomings.

For the new drophead model, the convertible hood was completely redesigned and greatly improved. The result was a hood that was much easier to operate and more effective. A smarter dashboard, 'luxuries' such as electric windows and improvements in overall finish, were also apparent. Special Equipment models of the drophead quickly followed; a 115 bhp engine, higher geared final drive, close-ratio gearbox and servo-assisted brakes all helped to make the Elan into an even faster sports car.

Production of Series 3 and Series 4 models totalled 2650 and nearly 3000 respectively.

Right
The S3 appeared in September 1965, although the S2 remained in production for a while. The S3 was available first only as a fixed head coupe and the example here is an American model. The black badge was introduced to mark the death of double Formula One world champion Jim Clark, who was killed outright after inexplicably crashing his Lotus 48 in a non-championship Formula Two race at Hockenheim, Germany on 7 April 1968. Clark's death devastated Colin Chapman, manager of Team Lotus, who – together with millions of motor sport enthusiasts – regarded him as a genius, one of the greatest racing drivers of all time. The black bumpers added to this car were a private change

Above

Along with the smart appearance of the fixed head coupe came improvements in the specification. Frames on the windows had increased rigidity and helped to restrict the draughts. The windows were also electrically controlled, although the cable mechanism was not particularly robust at first, resulting in slow operation and many breakdowns. On US export cars, the headlamp vacuum system was reversed so that if it failed the lights would automatically rise instead of retracting

Left

A Special Equipment model was announced in January 1966 for the S2 convertible and from July was available for the S3 FHC. Fitted with modified camshafts and re-jetted carburettors, the engine produced a claimed 115 bhp at 6000 rpm. The final drive ratio was raised from 3.9:1 to 3.77:1 for better cruising, whereas the close-ratio gearbox resulted in acceleration being much the same as previously. Servo-assisted brakes were standard on SE models

Left
In June 1966, the S3 convertible replaced the S2. By this time, the Elan had become a star of the small screen as the car driven by the leather-clad Emma Peel, played by Diana Rigg, in The Avengers TV series

Above
Along with the other benefits that came with the S3, the convertible had a greatly improved hood. The much simpler frame folded away with the cover on the shelf behind the seats

Above
When erected, the hood was now a much tighter and neater fit. With the window frames and better door seals, a considerably warmer and drier ride was possible

Left
The boot lid was extended over the rear of the car, thus eliminating the problem of water leaks into the boot. The car in the background is wearing its original colour of pistachio green. It is rarely seen these days, because although people regret not seeing it around, nobody seems to want their own car to be this colour

Left

The dash layout and instruments hardly changed, but the S4 introduced small fresh air vents at each end of the fascia, ventilated vinyl door and seat trims and flush BMC interior door handles as used on the Morris Marina, Austin Maxi, MGB, etc

Above

Solid-looking, streamlined mirrors were popular in the 1960s

Above
The pedal mechanism. The deep foot-well and the substantial range of seat adjustment available meant that even quite tall drivers could find a comfortable driving position

Right
The movement of the headlights was controlled by two vacuum cylinders powered by suction from the inlet manifold and with the aid of a vacuum reservoir in the chassis crossmember. If any leaks developed, the lights were prone to retract rather than remain up

Above
The next phase of styling changes came in March 1968, with the introduction of the S4. The body shell was somewhat thinner and lighter than on the S3

Left
With wider 155 x 13 tyres, slightly flared wheel arches became necessary. The Elan drew further praise for its handling qualities, being light and precise to drive. Side repeater flashers now became standard. This S4 is finished is French blue

Above

More modern looking and larger rear lights, similar to those on the Europa and Plus 2s, were fitted. Also evident here are the twin silencer pipes of the revised exhaust system and the spring clip which holds up the boot lid

Left

The dashboard had a lacquered walnut finish. It was made more comprehensive and featured modern rocker switches with identifying labels. This style of steering wheel displays Colin Chapman's signature, and was usually only seen on SE models

Above

The Zenith-Stromberg carbs were a little taller than the preceding Webers and a bonnet bulge was required to accommodate them. Despite being somewhat bigger than it really needed to be (or perhaps because it was), this 'power bulge' proved popular with some owners. Notwithstanding the Stromberg's undoubted merits, Lotus bowed to pressure from the majority of customers and reverted to Webers in October 1970

Right

A few early S4 engines were fitted with Weber carburettors but these were dropped in favour of twin Zenith-Stromberg 175CD carbs, which required a redesigned cylinder head casting. Stromberg-carburetted engines are identified by the high-level balance pipe and one piece air box – Weber and Dell'Orto carbs have a metal backplate and GRP air box. The Strombergs were supposedly introduced to meet strict American exhaust emission limits, but they tended to ice up and stick at very low temperatures. Although the power rating remained at 105 bhp, the carbs did give slightly better fuel consumption when cruising, albeit at the cost of some immediate throttle response. Modified camshafts were used to ensure no loss of power with the move away from Webers. The Special Equipment model was uprated to 118 bhp at 6000 rpm

The Sprint

The next upgrading of the Elan came in October 1970 in the form of the Sprint. By this time, Lotus was beginning to feel that the Elan was nearing the end of its natural life. Sales of the S4 had been slack and the main purpose of the Sprint was to revitalise sales, and the early models provided an opportunity to use up the many remaining parts by packaging them in a new, more attractive form.

To distinguish the new car from existing models, the Sprints were finished with gold bumpers, black wheels and a two-colour body. Performance was again increased with a new engine embossed with the words 'Big Valve'. Developed by Tony Rudd, formerly of BRM, engine modifications included larger inlet valves, high-lift cams and a higher compression ratio (from 9.5:1 to 10.3:1), giving an output of 126 bhp at 6500 rpm.

To complete the package, the transmission was strengthened to cope with the extra power. The changes certainly worked. The car was attractive and effective, fast and exciting to drive, with handling good enough and forgiving enough to cope with most drivers.

The last Elan rolled off the Hethel assembly line in August 1973. Nobody knows for certain how many Elans were made and any figures quoted may not be completely accurate, but it is generally accepted that about 1000 Sprints were manufactured, with very approximately around 8800 Elans being produced in total.

Left
Simply an S4 with increased performance, the 126 bhp 'big-valve' Sprint has since become the most desirable (and consequently the most expensive) of the road-going Elans. The owner, Paul Beedham, is seen here going for a spin among the hills of Derbyshire

Above.
This model is in the 'Gold Leaf' colours of carnival red and cirrus white. Sprints had Aztec gold bumpers and black wheels, although a few silver wheels were used up on the earlier models. All Sprints were sold as kits and none as factory-built cars. Rather pricey at £1700 as a kit and with no purchase tax, the Sprint was not a lot cheaper than a Jaguar E-type

Left
The main changes in the Sprint centred around the 'big-valve' engine. Featuring larger inlet valves and high-lift cams, compression ratio was raised from the 9.5:1 of earlier models to 10.3:1. Previously, the power ratings claimed for Elan were often considered to be a little optimistic, so Lotus was careful to release the accurate figures of 126 bhp at 6500 rpm and 113 lb/ft torque at 5500 rpm. In any event, the car now enjoyed a substantial increase in power. At the same time, the engine remained extremely flexible, being able to pull away smoothly from below 20 mph in top gear

Above

The Sprint brought a return of the Weber 40 DCOE carburettors, although they in turn were replaced by Dell'Orto carbs during the final months of production. This is an original and completely unused engine, fitted with Dell'Ortos and a five-speed box, on display in Mick Miller's workshop

Right

Some of the early Sprints were fitted with the bonnet bulge – a legacy of the Stromberg carburettor saga. Although Stromberg carbs were no longer being used, Lotus still had a number of bulged bonnets left over from S4 production and was simply using them up

Above and left
The new Sprint offered a considerable increase in power, achieving a top speed of 120 mph and a 0-60 time of 6.6 seconds. So be careful who offers you a lift. When the Sprint was first launched, the original literature announced a five-speed gearbox as an option. This would have been extremely useful for high speed cruising, but in fact it is believed that only three Sprints were fitted with five-speed gearboxes. These were added later by the service department to avoid the necessary type-approval tests

Above

One of the badges issued with the Sprint. On the other side, the badge lists Lotus' World Car Constructors Championship wins. One of the side repeater flashers may also be seen. This type was quite unusual at the time but more than one variety was used, depending on what supplies were available

Right

It would take a long search to find a better and more accurate engine bay than this example in Richard Wilson's Sprint as it nears completion

Above

The vent in the roof is to extract air from the cabin. It was only the very early fixed head coupes on the S3 that had no such vent

Right

The Sprint was available in both fixed head coupe drophead versions. This excellent paint job is the work of the car's owner, Neil Widdowson. It is in the original colour of colorado orange. Surprisingly, this warm and attractive colour is quite rare

Above

The small steering wheel and good seat adjustment allowed the driver to adopt the sporty straight-arm position. The door trim was identical to the S4's, with flush BMC-supplied interior door handles

Left

The increase in power required other modifications. The differential and drive shafts were strengthened, and a reinforcing bracket was added to the upper final drive mountings to cope with the extra torque. The Rotoflex doughnut joints were also stiffened, which reduced some of the surge motion caused by rapid acceleration

Above
The rear light cluster was also from the S4 and the number plate on this model is the original high relief type

Left
The 'Elan Sprint' strip down the length of the body was originally introduced to disguise the fact that the join between the two colours was often not particularly neat

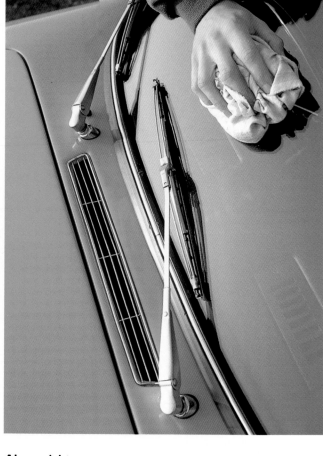

Above left

An original and rare jack. The Sprint's tyres, Dunlop SP Sports, as fitted here, were a textile braced radial particularly suited to the car, but are sadly no longer available

Above right

Another rare original item are these 'Speedblade' wipers, designed to reduce lifting at high speeds

Most Sprints came in two-tone, and strangely enough, any Sprints ordered in one just colour cost an extra £15. This example is in original condition and still runs extremely smoothly after 70,000 miles

Right

An extremely unusual Elan model is this estate made by Hexagon of North London and built to Sprint spec. Hexagon decided to make an estate in order to have larger carrying capacity and preferred the Elan to the Plus 2 because of its compactness, performance and agility. Plans, moulds and jigs were made and the intention was to produce a minimum of 50 vehicles. In the end, however, only two are believed to have been made. Although the idea of an Elan estate might sound a little strange, the design seems to work well

Above

The roof is double skinned and is bonded on, and contains a layer of polyurethane foam. Rams from the Renault 12 Estate give support to the rear door. The rear window is heated and features a wiper and electric wash. It offered a considerable increase in luggage space, although the suspension turrets did restrict the size of the interior a little. Overall weight increase was 42 lb and the handling is claimed to be unaffected by the modification

On the track

Colin Chapman had not envisaged the Elan as a racing car and at first was not interested in developing it as such. Racing enthusiasts had other ideas, however. When the Elan came on the market in 1962, it was soon apparent that it was going to be ideally suited to the track; the car handled superbly and the engine had plenty of racing potential. Being a relatively simple car and easy to work on, club racers could undertake modifications in progressive stages. Lighter and more basic, without the improvements in trim incorporated on later models, the S1 and S2 were more readily adaptable and, not surprisingly, proved to be particularly popular. Even so, the standard car was not completely suited for competition without modifications.

The Chequered Flag, a company based in Chobham, Surrey run by Graham Warner, played a significant role in modifying the Elan to meet the demands of the racing circuit. Changes included wider tyres, adjustable (and uprated) suspension, racing springs and dampers, anti-roll bars front and rear, substituting roller splines in the drive shafts instead of the standard rubber doughnuts, and mounting the radiator further forward. In addition, the vacuum-operated pop-up headlights were replaced by small headlights mounted behind perspex covers to save valuable weight. Engine modifications delivered a lusty 145 bhp at 7000 rpm.

Graham Warner was by no means the only exponent in this area: in the 1963 season his car battled against the special-bodied Elan owned by Stirling Moss's SMART racing team and usually driven by John Whitmore. Unmistakable in British 'Vomit' Green, the SMART Elan suffered the ignominy of losing a wheel in two of the races it entered, but was otherwise totally reliable. Racing Elans soon appeared with alloy wheels

Left

An S1 in full flight around a wet Mallory Park circuit. Most racing Elans were fitted with the standard hard top, although some owners got away with leaving the cloth hood up according to how the GT regulations were interpreted. In the early days of Elan racing, the tried and tested Elite tended to be more reliable, but by August 1963 the young pretender was taking over in long distance events such as the Tourist Trophy at Goodwood. The following year 1600 cc Elans dominated the small GT class, previously a happy hunting ground for the Elite. At Mallory Park back in May 1964, future Formula One world champion Jackie Stewart led a 1-2-3 Elan procession over the finishing line when his Chequered Flag-prepared car beat Peter Arundell driving Ian Walker's well-known 'Gold Bug'

Above

Photographed at the 1964 Le Mans 24 Hours is the 26R of Richard Gele; Team Lotus entered a 26R driven by Jackie Oliver. Other famous drivers associated with the car included Jackie Stewart, Stirling Moss, Jochen Rindt and Jim Clark. Rindt was given a 126 hp big-valve Sprint as his personal road, but sadly had little time to enjoy it before he became Lotus's posthumous Formula One world champion in 1970. Based at Bourne in Lincolnshire, BRM offered four states of tune for the 26R: Phase I gave 130-140 bhp; Phase II gave 140+ bhp; Phase III gave 160+ bhp with Weber carbs; while Phase IV promised (but apparently never delivered) 175+ bhp with fuel injection

Left

Robin Longdon enjoying himself in a Type 26R. One person who certainly knows about driving the BRM-powered Elan (for Willment Racing) is John Miles, who won every race at the 1966 Goodwood Easter meeting in a 135 bhp 26R Series II and went on to win the Autosport Championship; by the end of the season Willment's had raised peak power to 155 bhp at 7000 rpm. The faired-in front bumper, perspex headlight covers, slightly flared wheel arches, and J A Pearce alloy wheels characterise the genuine article. John Miles' distinguished racing career ended when he left the Lotus grand prix team in 1970. After 'Miles behind the wheel' as the technical editor of the weekly magazine Autocar, he returned to Lotus in 1984; together with Roger Becker, Miles became a leading advocate of front-wheel-drive for the new Elan

instead of the standard steel items.

Very quickly, some of the changes being made by engine and race preparation specialists were imitated by Lotus, who produced their own racing version of the Elan in 1964 designated Type 26R – '26' being the model designation of the S1 and S2 cars, with the 'R' for racing. As Cosworth (who built and supplied all Lotus racing engines) were overloaded with work at the time, BRM received the contract to prepare every Elan 26R engine. BRM enlarged the twin-cam Coventry Climax FPF unit to 1594 cc, boosting output to around 160 bhp in Phase III form with Weber carburettors; it incorporated BRM-designed crankshafts, con-rods, and pistons, and the company fitted bigger valves and gas-flowed and ported the cylinder heads. Stronger, sand-cast heads came from William Mills, although the standard Cooper head gasket was retained. The chassis was strengthened to carry the lightweight glassfibre body, and weight was also saved by using magnesium alloy for the wheels and final drive casing. The suspension was stiffened and lowered, and to accommodate wider racing tyres, new wheel arches were added. A limited slip differential enhanced power transfer and some cars had a variable cooling system with its own oil pump. Properly sorted, the Type 26R was certainly the car to beat...

Left
This attractive engine bay would do credit to any concours event. In fact it is a car being prepared by Tony Thompson Racing for some hard campaigning in Europe.

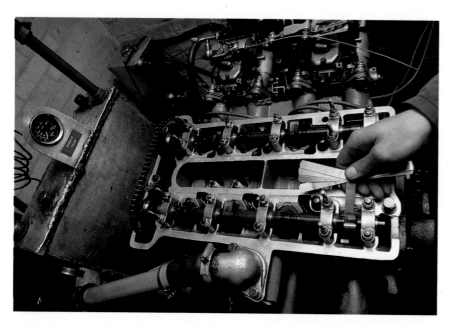

Above

On the test bench at Quorn Engine Developments is a racing engine with high-lift cams. The twin-cam race engine is completely different from the road engine, a number of specialised high performance components (such as racing pistons with steel main caps and a fully balanced crankshaft) being added to the basic cylinder block and head. Maximum torque will be at about 6500 rpm and maximum power in the region of 7500 rpm. The chain driving the twin overhead cams is clearly visible

Right

One of the current big names in Elan racing is Tony Thompson. In the foreground, in his workshop, is the genuine 26R in which he regularly competes in historic sports car races throughout Europe. Extremely competitive in their class, genuine 26Rs are still hard to beat. It is quite possible to construct a replica 26R and attempts have been made to pass them off as the real thing. Apart from their BRM-Lotus engines, the 26R had wider wheels, rose-jointed suspension, dual-circuit braking, a stiffened chassis and a lighter body shell. Officially, 52 were made in the S1 series and 45 in the S2. Accurate production figures are hard to find – it was not uncommon for Lotus to sell Elans 'under the counter' for cash and these cars do not appear in any records. Only about 30 genuine Type 26Rs are definitely known to survive today

Above
Starting life as standard road cars, these two were converted to lightweight racing
Elans. The radiator has been moved forward to improve cooling

Above right
Chris Reece in action in his race prepared lightweight. An air scoop is fitted to cool the
final drive

Right
Andi Gregoire of France in a race-prapared Elan with Le Mans lights

Left
One of the beauties of the Elan is the fact that the standard car can be put on the track providing tremendous fun for the participant. Modifications can be made in a piecemeal manner as circumstances allow

Above
The Elan is also a very competitive car when it comes to hill-climbing. Its rapid acceleration and sharp handling make it a good choice for such events

Above

Shapecraft made about ten of these fastback models, all of S1 vintage. Usually their special roofs – sometimes with louvres and side rear windows – were mounted on 26R bodies. Les Arnold had two works Shapecraft cars, producing 145 bhp in 1964 and 170 bhp in 1965. In 1970, the Shapecraft S1 was declared illegal because it had not been homologated. Only about six examples are believed to survive

Left

Almost receiving a broadside is an Elan in the BRM colours of polychromatic dark green with blaze orange bumpers. BRM's works car was driven by Mike Spence, whose Maidenhead, Berks-based company offered a range of BRM engine modifications and optional extras for the Elan and Elan SE. The 'Mike Spence' Lotus Elan BRMs (approximately 20 built during 1967) had 140 bhp high compression engines with fully balanced conrods and either a Cosworth CPL2 crankshaft (road use) or L1 (for competition only). Other changes included a better oil pump, different chokes and jets and a choice of exhaust systems, namely a fabricated four branch manifold with large diameter pipe and Elan SE silencer, or a Jaguar E-type straight through silencer for racing. As tested by Autosport, the Lotus Elan BRM Special Equipment (priced at £1650 in component form) recorded a top speed of 130 mph, the 0-60 dash being achieved in 6.8 seconds and the standing quarter mile in 15.1 seconds – performance on a par with most racing cars and comparable to the larger Aston Martin DB6 Vantage and Jaguar E-type. The Stage III-tuned Ian Walker Elan coupe conversion offered in October 1966 was also extremely quick, its 135 bhp engine accelerating the car from rest to 100 mph in 17 seconds

Left and above

Lotus supplied just one of these fastback cars – with an aluminium top. The body was made by Williams and Pritchard and the car went to Ian Walker Racing. Its first driver was Jackie Stewart in the 'Shake-down Races'. The intention was to race the car in the 1965 Le Mans, but a week before the race Mike Spence overturned it damaging the roof so badly that the car missed the race. It has a 26R chassis and suspension, magnesium wheels and a 1800 cc twin cam engine. It is owned and driven by Paul Matty

Part of the collection of long-term Lotus enthusiast, Malcolm Ricketts. From the left is a replica 26R, an S2 road car developed for post-historic racing, and an original Sprint ELA 111 fitted with the later indicator reflectors

The Elan Plus 2

Above

The Elan Plus 2 (written '+2' on the car's badge), was first introduced in June 1967. Compared the standard Elan, the doors on the Plus 2 were wider to allow access to the rear seats. They were also thicker and stronger, while steel stiffeners were fitted into the door sills. As well as strengthening the car in the event of a side impact, they were used for attaching the seat belts and as jacking points

Right

The overall dimensions of the Plus 2 were greater than the Elan all round, being 23 inches longer, ten inches wider and two inches higher. At first, the Plus 2 could be purchased in kit form or as a finished car. Featuring the Elan SE engine generating 115 bhp at 6000 rpm, the Plus 2 could achieve 0-60 in 9 seconds and had a top speed of 120 mph. The longer body improved the aerodynamics; the 0.34 Cd of the Elan was now lowered to 0.32 on the Plus 2

The concept of producing a more luxurious and roomier version of the Elan had been around for some time, but with the introduction of the Elan coupe in 1964, the Plus 2 took second place. Further delays were caused by improved sales of the Elan and the pending move to the new factory at Hethel, Norfolk. In fact, this all worked to the advantage of the Plus 2 because it enabled more development work to take place. The Elan Plus 2 was part of the Lotus plan to go up-market with a more refined, sophisticated car. With this in mind, the Plus 2 was styled to have both a sports and saloon car appearance. The two small rear seats made the car a suitable choice for the family man, so that he could now take the children along, or not escape from them, depending on your point of view. The interior trim, with the luxurious seats and elaborate dashboard, helped to further the more up-market image. After the basic model, it was not long before improvements came along, in the form of increased performance and more distinctive paint finishes. The top-of-the-range Elan Plus 2 was designated the 130/5, which came with a useful fifth gear for relaxed high-speed cruising.

A total of 3300 Elan Plus 2s had been produced when the last 130/5 was built in December 1974. Thereafter, Lotus concentrated on producing a series of dramatically styled, luxurious sports cars such as the new Elite, Esprit and Eclat until the new Elan was launched in October 1989.

Left
The Plus 2 range was aimed at a more sophisticated market than the purely sporty Elan, although there were many similarities between the models. The backbone chassis was successfully extended to accommodate the longer body. The suspension system and drivetrain were also similar to the Elan's, with some common parts. With the weight increased to 17 cwt, the springs and dampers were uprated accordingly. Ten inch-diameter servo-assisted disc brakes gave the Plus 2 even greater stopping power than the already impressive Elan

Above

As with the standard Elan, Lotus continually refined and improved its bigger brother: the Plus 2S appeared in March 1969, complete with Zenith-Stromberg carburettors and associated bonnet bulge. Power was upped slightly to 118 bhp and more luxury touches were added in the cabin. The Plus 2S was only available as a complete car and thus became the first Lotus never sold in kit form – a significant departure. The company made a determined effort to improve the general build quality of the Plus 2 series to enhance its appeal in an increasingly decerning market. Fitted with the 126 bhp big valve engine from the Sprint, the wickedly quick Plus 2S 130 became available in October 1970. All the 130s had silver roofs, as displayed by this otherwise metallic lagoon blue example

Above right

As previously mentioned, the practice of sourcing components from other car manufacturers continued with the Plus 2. The front bumper came from the Ford Anglia and was fitted upside-down, whereas the rear bumper came from the BMC Riley Elf/Wolseley Hornet and had an extra piece grafted in the middle. The Ford 'parts bin' was also raided for the windscreen glass and surrounding steel pressing (Capri), while the tail lamps were the later Elan fitting turned upside-down. Incidentally, Colin Chapman had never liked the glassfibre reinforced plastic bumpers (another Ron Hickman innovation) fitted to the Elan, and he insisted on chrome bumpers for the Plus 2 series

Right

The upgraded Plus 2S 130 was, in effect, the Elan Sprint for the family man. The drive shafts and Rotoflex couplings were strengthened to deliver the engine's 126 bhp to the road as efficiently as possible. The powerplant retained the enlarged inlet valves and sharper camshafts developed for the Elan Sprint by Tony Rudd, Lotus's engineering director

Above
The knock-off wheels came with 165 radials

Right
The pop-up headlights were placed more inboard than on the two-seater Elans –
when raised the lights had a detrimental effect on the styling and aerodynamics

Overleaf
The low and elegant profile of what was destined to be the last Plus 2 model: the
130/5. Available from October 1972, the 130/5 featured a five-speed gearbox (an
Austin Maxi derived unit with a Lotus aluminium casing) with top gear adjusted for
cruising rather than increased performance; top speed remained 120 mph, but was
achieved at 1300 rpm lower than the four-speed models

Above

More luxurious trim was an important feature of the Plus 2 range; covered in Ambla, the well shaped seats gave firm support. The rear seats were best suited for children and so the car became ideal for the family man who still wanted to drive a sports car. This Plus 2S 130/5 features oatmeal trim

Left

The new burr walnut veneer dashboard was considerably more elaborate than on the Elan. Its smart, clear layout epitomised the more up-market image Lotus was striving for. As well as the normal array of facilities, there was an outside-temperature gauge and, unusual at the time, a map reading light. The radio fitted to this car is non-standard. Additional niceties included lights under the bonnet and boot and red warning lights on the open doors. I wonder how many well-heeled owners realised that the air vents, indicator stalk, handbrake, cigar lighter and sun visors all came from the Ford Cortina Mk 2 family saloon?

Above

A rare car at any competitive event is a Plus 2...

Left

...even rarer is Plus 2 convertible. No convertible Plus 2s ever rolled off the Lotus production line, but a number have been converted privately

Above

The distinctive colour scheme was black with metal flake gold roof and gold coach line

Left

To celebrate their 50th Grand Prix victory, Lotus brought out a commemorative Plus 2 model painted in John Player Special colours; they have since become rather rare cars. This fine example is number 84 of the 85 made and is owned by Roy Palmer. The exemplary handling of the Plus 2 certainly impressed its owners. The steering was light and responsive and gave the drive of a sports car combined with the comfort and space normally associated with saloon cars

LIMITED EDITION TO COMMEMORATE
FIRST 50 LOTUS GRAND PRIX WINS

Left
The sill of the JPS Plus 2 was also finished in gold and the right wing sported the commemorative plaque

Above
Roy Palmer has kept his JPS Plus 2 standard throughout, apart from the indulgence of an F1 model on the dashboard

Restoration

Left

Bodyshell restoration: new tissue or mat is laid on to the damaged area and the resin worked well in from the centre outwards. Extra mat can be put under the wheel arches and on areas requiring reinforcement. An electric sander is then used in the first stage of smoothing. The shell is then flatted by hand with progressively finer grades of Wet & Dry paper. Thorough drying is essential here, as any moisture trapped in the fibres will eventually cause the paint to blister

Below

Two or three layers of polyester filler are sprayed on to give a good body contour. The shell should be left to dry for several days in a dry environment or placed in a heated booth before sanding

Rare indeed is the Elan that does not require some restoration work. To make matters worse, it is not uncommon to find a 'bodged' Elan in which expedient or downright poor bodywork repairs have been disguised with a fresh coat of paint. In addition, most cars need regular and professional maintenance of their mechanical components to keep them in good running order, but this is especially true of the Elan.

What first meets the eye, of course, is the bodywork and the glassfibre is prone to a number of problems. The gel was applied in the original mould, where it hardened to form a smooth surface for the paint and prevented the glassfibre from absorbing solvents. The trouble is, the gel is brittle and prone to cracking and, once removed, it cannot be replaced with new gel. Star fractures in the gel are caused by impacts from underneath the car, usually from stones striking the wheel arches. Fractures also occur at stress points such as the fixing for the door hinges and handles, and around corners. Long cracks in the body panels are the result of the car flexing under strain.

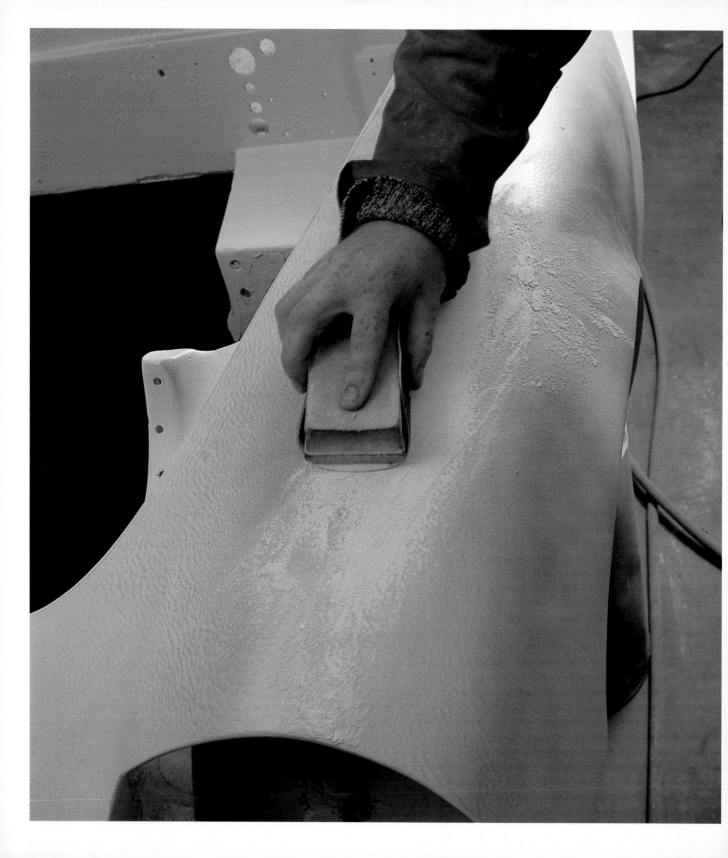

Left

Flatting is done by hand with progessively finer grades of dry paper; a light guide spray coat of paint will reveal any discrepancies in the contours

Above

A polyurethane epoxy is used on the filler as a sealer and the modern two-pack paints also form a good barrier on the glassfibre because they dry by chemical reaction. Three undercoats of high-build primer are followed by six to eight top coats. The two-pack paints contain isocyanates and must only be used when wearing a breathing mask in a proper ventilated and filtered spray booth. The shell featured in this photograph is in the SMS workshop. Ideally, the paint is flatted between coats with very fine grades, and after being finally flatted it is buffed and polished. A full body respray for an Elan takes a long time and has to done exactly right, so it's hardly surprising that most owners turn pale when they receive the quote for the job from a professional restorer. New doors, bonnets and boots will require fine adjustment to fit perfectly – protruding door bottoms are a common problem

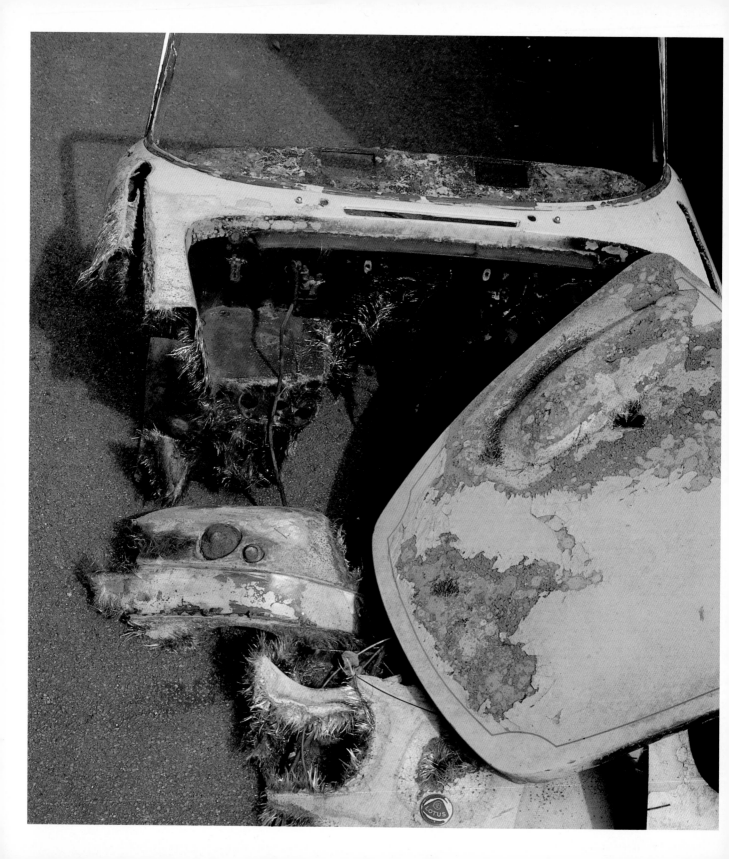

Left

Fires are not uncommon with the Elan. The ignition coil is under the carbs and a petrol leak is potentially extremely serious. In addition, the removal of the air box can allow the carburettor to spit back and catch fire

Above

Richard Wilson bought his Sprint after it suffered an accidental fire. After grafting on a new front end, he was brave enough to undertake his own respray, with excellent results. An underseal of Bitumastic is useful to help prevent star cracking from underneath the body shell

Whether one is correcting such faults, repairing crash damage or undertaking a complete respray, the procedure is much the same and careful preparation is all important. Normal paint strippers tend to be too strong and will damage the gel coat, so the usual method of removing old paint is to carefully scrape it away with a chisel. Any remaining paint may be removed using Wet & Dry paper, allowing the quality of previous repairs and the condition of the gel coat to be properly examined and assessed. Fine gel cracks can be hard to find but a wipe over with a damp cloth will help to reveal them. Damaged areas need to be cleaned carefully with an angle grinder before the edges are finally blended in by hand.

Left

It makes no sense at all to repair an old chassis. If there are any signs whatever of cracks, damage, rust or fatigue, the risks are too great. New chassis are readily available from the factory at a reasonable price and are actually better protected than the originals. An early chassis was only painted with red oxide and bitumen, whereas the modern version is galvanised and considerably better protected against the elements. In the past, Lotus failed to meet the demand for spares and were in fact known to be actually destroying parts and production jigs. Consequently, many small independent firms sprang up to supply a range of Elan components. Today, things have changed for the better and the factory spares position for the Elan is now really very good, more comfortable than it is for many other classic cars

Above

The standard Mk 2 crankshaft; an EN40B steel crank for racing and good for 8500 rpm (the holes are for oil flow and balancing); and a forged billet prior to machining

Left

The engines fitted to the first Elans produced only modest power compared with the later big-valve models and some of the components were not able to withstand the increase in output. The early conrods, for example, were just able to cope in a standard engine, but would break when subjected to greater power and higher revs. Similarly, the early main bearing caps were not designed to survive the forces generated by uprated engines. The three pistons shown here are high performance (top), high compression (left) and standard

Above

Mick Miller is working here on a brace of Sprints in his Suffolk workshop. A long established Elan restorer, Mick Miller has been in the business since Elans first went into production

Above left

A standard twin-cam engine prepared by QED. The green cam cover usually denotes a Special Equipment engine from around 1966

Right

A big-valve engine mounted on the chassis and ready to receive the body shell. Some of the complaints about the Elan engine, such as excessive oil leaks and timing chain failure, are invariably caused by poor maintenance. An over tightened fan belt, for example, will lead to water pump failure

The new Elan

After false starts with two previous concepts of the new Elan, which failed to reach production due to lack of money, the rebirth of the Elan was heralded by the takeover of Group Lotus by the American car giant General Motors on 14 January 1986. The Group Lotus' board of directors approved the design of the new Elan (principally the work of Peter Stevens) in November that year, and prototype number 103 of the M100 (as the new car was code-named) was let loose onto the Hethel test track on 16 November 1987 – under cover of darkness to foil any journalistic scoops.

Despite intense media interest, Lotus managed to keep the final shape of the car secret until March 1988, when *Car* magazine splashed a photograph of the full-size silver model on its front cover. Another 'own goal' was scored on February 1989, when a photographer chanced upon a pair of development vehicles parked at Harwich dockyard before they sailed to Sweden for validation and winter testing; his pictures gave *Autocar & Motor* an exclusive on 8 March 1989. Their appetites well and truly whetted, Lotus fans could hardly wait for the launch of the new Elan, and when it was announced at the London Motorfair in October 1989 – 27 years after the public debut of the original Elan – they were generally enthusiastic.

Resurrecting such a deified name was not only logical – both Elans were two-seater high performance sports cars with glassfibre bodies and a backbone chassis – but also good marketing. At around £20,000 a copy, Lotus claimed that the first year of UK production was sold during the car's ten-day stay at Motorfair. The first production Elans were delivered to customers in April 1990.

Coincidentally (and rather ominously), the Mazda MX-5 was launched shortly before the new Elan. Often described as an updated clone of the

Right

The new Elan's multi-panelled composite body reflects the revolution in glassfibre construction since the early sixties. Lotus's patented Vacuum Assisted Resin Injection (VARI) process was used to manufacture the car's 63 composite body panels; each piece of glassfibre was preformed before being moulded into its final shape by a secret method which Lotus calls Fibreform. The high-gloss paint finish is in a different class from the old 'cut and polish' of earlier Lotus glassfibre cars; after priming, four coats of ICI two-pack acrylic-polyurethane paint were spayed on by hand and, after flashing and lacquering, the bodyshell was oven baked for 80 minutes at 80°C. The resultant lustrous sheen is as good as any achieved on a steel-bodied car

Above

The new Elan was only available as a convertible, the soft top being a particularly neat design developed by Tickford in Milton Keyes and manufactured at the company's Bedworth plant. The roof stowage cover, situated immediately forward of the boot lid, is unlatched by operating the release handle located in the offside door jamb. Although not power operated, the hood can be easily erected in a few seconds and is designed to fold down in one continuous movement. A pair of over-centre latch fittings attach the hood to the windscreen header rail

Left

A major departure was the front-wheel-drive layout, which required new technology and changes in suspension construction. The front suspension has double wishbones attached to a cast aluminium 'raft', a patented innovation developed at Lotus by John Miles and Jerry Booen. This in turn is mounted on the chassis longeron with three rubber bushes (the design of which is unique to the Elan), which help to isolate suspension shocks and maintain instant steering response. The raft keeps the car glued to the road while minimising vibration – a major contribution to the Elan's amazing ride and handling. Coaxial coil springs and dampers are attached to the front chassis longeron at the top end. At the bottom end, the lower wishbone (main member) absorbs the torque through the driving wheels. The anti-roll bar is attached by a drop link from each chassis longeron. The rear suspension is attached to the backbone chassis via a rear crossmember and has a single wide-based lower wishbone with diagonal linkage which, along with stiffer wishbone bushes, controls the movement of the rear wheels to prevent front wheel dive and rear end lift under heavy braking. The rear arm of the wishbone is attached to a rearward extension from the chassis backbone. An anti-roll bar is also fitted on the rear, drop linked from the rear crossmember

original Elan, the MX-5 is beautifully made and tremendous fun to drive. In terms of absolute performance and handling, the MX-5 is obviously outclassed by the turbocharged Elan SE; but priced at around £15,000 in the UK, the Japanese pretender rapidly became the world's best selling two-seater sports car. Even before the economic recession had begun to bite, the 'hot hatch' brigade of XR3i, Golf GTI and 205GTI owners tempted to buy an open sports car deserted the new Elan in droves in favour of the much cheaper (and better looking?) MX-5. Drivers 'trading down' from the Porsche 924/944 and Toyota Celica/Supra also found the MX-5 irresistible. And in the United States, a make-or-break market for Lotus, the MX-5 (marketed as the Miata) was a car salesman's dream come true. By the beginning of 1992, when even large discounts on its $39,000 price tag failed to tempt American buyers, the new Elan began to look very vulnerable indeed.

Even so, the news that Elan production would end in June 1992 came as a considerable shock. Surely a company backed by the mighty GM could afford to support such a technically brilliant car until sales recovered? Apparently not. A company spokesman stated that even if they produced the planned 3000 cars a year, the Elan would still not make a profit. Lotus cut their losses and closed the Elan production line as planned to concentrate on the Esprit, which continues to make money. With the wisdom of hindsight, perhaps Lotus was wrong to view the Elan as such a low volume car? Pricing naturally had to take account of development costs, but increasing the production rate would have reduced the price of the Elan and extended its market base. Putting such speculation aside, it seems most unlikely that the Elan name will be used again.

A grand total of 3857 new Elans were built, all but 180 being the turbocharged SE model.

Right

The new Elan is powered by a 1.6-litre 'Isuzu-Lotus' 4XE1 four-cylinder, 16-valve engine fitted with electronic multi-point fuel injection. The aluminium alloy cylinder head incorporates belt-driven double overhead camshafts. The normally aspirated (NA) model delivers 130 bhp at 7200 rpm and 105 lb/ft torque at 4200 rpm. However, 95 per cent of purchasers opted for the turbocharged Elan SE, for which the corresponding figures are 165 bhp at 6600 rpm and 148 lb/ft at 4200 rpm. The Elan SE accelerates from 0-60 mph in 6.7 seconds and has a top speed of 137 mph. Other SE performance figures include despatching the standing quarter-mile in 15 seconds (terminal speed 92 mph), while the standing kilometre takes 27.4 seconds (terminal speed 118 mph). Overall fuel consumption of the turbo is similar to the NA version at 26 mpg – the same as the old Elan – although over 40 mpg is possible for the economy-minded. Both cars have a petrol tank capacity of 10.2 gallons. The first Isuzu engines were fitted in two X100 prototypes in April 1987, the 1.6-litre Toyota Corolla powertrain having been previously used for front-wheel-drive development since early 1985

Above

Once in place, the roof is tight and firm and generates surprisingly little wind noise, even at speeds approaching 100 mph – a tribute to its streamlining. The car's Cd is reduced to 0.34 with the hood up, compared to 0.38 with the hood down. It is made of triple-layer black fabric with a cotton lining and is attached to an epoxy powder-coated steel frame with spring assistance. Rear view is maintained through a single plastic window. One old problem was never completely cured, however, as the hood tended to leak in heavy rain. This car is finished in Norfolk mustard

Right

The overall appearance of the new Elan was generally popular, looking particularly good from the front and the rear. In profile, perhaps the front end looked a little short and stubby. The styling saga of the new Elan began in the mid 1970s, when Oliver Winterbottom, who had earlier styled the Elite, spent three years working on the initial rear-wheel-drive M90 Elan concept. Only one M90, powered by a Toyota 1.6-litre engine, was made and the project was abandoned in favour of the X100 in 1985. Peter Stevens' first proposal for the X100 appeared in one-fifth scale model form in early 1984 and a full-size version was later created by CECOMP of Turin. The first X100 prototype was driven on the Hethel test track in January 1986, but further development had already been on hold since December 1985. Italian master-stylist Giugiaro and GM both submitted full-size models of the subsequent M100 in November 1986; Stevens' winning proposal (slightly altered by production engineering) is the Elan we see today. Stevens also styled the seven-spoke 15-inch alloy wheels manufactured by OZ of Italy

Above left
The roomy interior is bold in concept, although the predominance of dark grey leather-grained 'slush' mouldings on the main fascia were not to everyone's taste. GM supplied the instrument pack. A nice touch is the interior illumination provided by two small lights in the base of the rear view mirror. The lockable glovebox is opened by its own key. Most SE models were delivered with optional two-tone grey full leather seat facings and door inserts shown here. The leather-trimmed steering wheel is adjusted for height by a clamp lever on the left-hand side of the column. The seats give a firm yet comfortable ride; 'LOTUS' is embossed in the backrest

Left
The Elan was an all-new design – apart from the famous badge nothing came from another Lotus. But not surprisingly, some proprietary parts were sourced from 'big brother' GM, including (with minor modifications in some cases) rear stud axles, wheel bearings, and front hubs and brakes from the Vauxhall Cavalier/Opel Ascona. A factory hard-top was displayed in October 1991 at the Earls Court Motorfair, and had production continued it could have been optioned or retrofitted to any Elan from August 1992 (Photo: Richard Newton)

Above
The rear end looks purposeful and exudes power. This view shows the integrated spoiler design, SE badging and the perspex number plate cover. The tail lamp clusters came from the Renault GTA. US models differ in having an integral rear wing with altered boot lid opening, and 16 inch wheels with smaller slots